IT HAPPENED ON OUR WATCH

TINA JONES WILLIAMS

It Happened on Our Watch

Copyright 2020

Tina Jones Williams

Bibliographical Data:

Williams, Tina Jones

ISBN: 9798542108063

General Fiction

PREFACE

"We do not write to be understood; we write to
understand." C. Day-Lewis

PROLOGUE

It was Berkeley in the late 60s and we wore our Blackness as a mantel. We wore dashikis, African dresses, African jewelry, meticulous afros, and elaborate braids. We celebrated and reveled in our Blackness. But it was short-lived. Too soon, when we graduated from high school and later some of us from college, we got real jobs. And for acceptance, we traded our dashikis and African dresses for two-piece skirt-suits or blazers and well-fitting slacks. We set aside our African jewelry for small gold hoops or even smaller gold studs and barely-there gold pendants. We replaced our afros and braids with the corporate haircut and settled into our sameness. With our sameness came a shift. Was it an undetectable decline? Or was it a freefall when the stars misaligned? Either way, it happened on our watch.

SOMEWHERE ALONG THE WAY

Ours was the Affirmative Action generation. We had opportunities our parents could have only dreamed of. We graduated from high school in record numbers. Right out of high school some joined major corporations and took on professional jobs on a career track. Others went to college where they completed undergraduate and advanced degrees foundational to secure their future. We flourished in our chosen careers. By our parents' yardstick we had unmeasured success. We were held up as shining examples of what was possible.

We made good matches, got married and bought homes in the best neighborhoods that money could buy. Some had the requisite 2.5 children. They were nurtured, groomed, and sent to the best schools that money could buy. We joined or reconfirmed our commitment to groups, African American Churches, Sororities and Fraternities, Jack and Jill, Links, and all the others. If we didn't become members, at the very least we affiliated. All done so that our children would be equipped with a full tool kit to successfully navigate the future we planned for them.

In every arena that mattered, our generation thrived, and in every arena that mattered we were accepted with opened arms. Or so we thought. But, somewhere along the way, despite doing all the right things, our carefully crafted life began to show cracks in its facade. Mounting evidence told us maybe we weren't so special. Despite deliberate navigation, the life we had so carefully steered in the right direction began to veer off course. Mounting evidence began to tell us maybe we were not so universally accepted. Doubt began to creep in. We began to silently wonder if our children would be viewed as relatable, universally accepted. We silently wondered if the life we had planned for our children even existed. Worst yet we silently wondered if they would even want it.

Should we have seen this seismic shift coming? We couldn't have. Our faith, hopes, dreams, and self-preserving little white lies rendered our version of the future unreliable at best and a cautionary tale at worst. Only if we had allowed ourselves to see unvarnished truth through an unbiased lens, within a stark context, could we have seen it coming. But only if we hadn't pulled the wool over our own eyes.

WHAT THEY WISHED FOR, WHAT
THEY GOT

THEN. 1943

My father got to Berkeley first, leaving the family behind in Chicago. He settled in a South Berkeley boarding house, somewhere near Harmon Street and Adeline Avenue. Many of the homes in the area had been converted into boarding houses to accommodate Colored people new in town and Pullman porters who traveled extensively. Not being able to find work as a carpenter, he took a job at the Richmond Shipyards. It was during WWII and most Colored wage earners in Berkeley and the surrounding areas were employed by the government in some capacity in support of the war effort.

After several months of getting acclimated to a city where he knew no one and where he had never been before, my dad was ready for my mother and my siblings to join him. On a segregated train ride from Chicago to Berkeley, my mother spent three days and two nights traveling with three of my older siblings, my brother an infant, another brother almost three years old, and my sister, the oldest, who was not yet four. I can only imagine the complicated logistics, challenges, and bouts of doubt she must have faced on that cross-country ride. Once in Berkeley, with the whole family together, in a multi-family boarding house, in unfamiliar surroundings, sharing two rooms, I suspect the reality of the move settled in quickly.

In fall of 1943 my mother was twenty-three and my father was twenty-five, and as I mentioned they had three children aged four and under. On faith they had left the South side of Chicago and the comfort of family and familiarity to seek equality and greater opportunity in Berkeley, California. What they wished for and what they got were totally different. They had hoped to leave unfair employment practices, segregated housing, and separate and unequal education behind, but they found it all waiting for them in South Berkeley.

Like my father, my mother was hired at the Richmond Shipyards. She was a welder along with many others, building war ships for immediate use. The Shipyards operated three eight hour shifts seven days a week. The working conditions were harsh, and the treatment of Colored people was harsher, they were not wanted but they were needed. To be hired there was a strict pecking order, first hired were White males who were not eligible for the armed services, next in line to be hired were White women, then Black men, who were hired to do jobs White women didn't want to do or couldn't do, and last hired were Black women. In many cases though their duties were the same, White women refused to work with or near Black women. Like so many other indignities they suffered, that's just the way it was.

After months in Berkeley living in the boarding house,

my parents found and finalized the purchase of their forever home on Julia Street, north of Harmon Street but still in South Berkeley. What they didn't know when they made the decision to move from the segregated South side of Chicago to Berkeley, was that Berkeley was also segregated. People of color, including Asians and Hispanics were not welcomed to rent or buy homes outside of the contrived borders of South Berkeley. The boundaries are Grove Street, now MLK, and Dwight Way. The redlined borders were strictly enforced by real estate agents who adhered to written covenants and verbal "gentlemen's agreements."

In the late fall of 1943, my family moved into their brand new but modest home. The purchase price was $5,000.00. The home was single story, a small footprint on a generous lot. It featured two bedrooms and one bathroom. When they bought the property my father, a skilled carpenter, had plans to add a second story to the family home and build apartments in back. He always said the additions were intended to house and support the growing family.

My mother always remarked that the neighborhood felt familiar, and their neighbors were welcoming. Homes were well maintained, and yards were well kept. Businesses, only steps away on Sacramento Street were Colored owned, like the homes in the area. My family had found their place. They made friends quickly and became part of the neighborhood.

TALENT AND PERSISTENCE

1945

In 1945 WWII ended and my older sister was born. The birth of my sister evened the scales. At that point there were two boys and two girls, according to my mother a perfectly matched set. At the end of the war my father joined the Carpenters' Union in Berkeley where dues were paid, information disseminated, and jobs secured. The hiring process for union carpenters was supposed to be seniority driven, but the reality was the process was driven by race first and seniority second. According to my father, that's just the way it was.

Due to talent and persistence, and despite the flawed system, my father had little trouble getting work. Over the years he worked on residential and commercial projects throughout the Bay Area. Most of his jobs were in segregated neighborhoods in the Berkeley and Oakland hills. White neighborhoods were where the opportunity was. He was grateful for the opportunities, but they did not come without strings attached. Whenever he worked in the Berkeley or Oakland hills, he was stopped by the police almost every morning and asked what he was doing in the area. Because it was a ritual, he left early enough to make time for the daily routine. There was nothing to be done about it except to find a work around, find ways to mitigate it, because that's just the way it was.

From the beginning the home on Julia Street, with just one bath and two bedrooms, was too small for our family. To make room for everyone, my parents designed plans and my father built a second story with additional bedrooms and an additional bathroom. Taking advantage of the area behind the family home my father left space for a small backyard, added a detached cottage and a duplex. My mother told the story of how my father, with city approved plans in hand, went from one bank to another to secure a loan to build the project. He was turned down at each one. When he had had enough, he told my mother "I will build it if I have to pay for it one nail at a time." And he did. It's likely I was a toddler the first time I heard that story.

In the fall of the same year my two oldest siblings along with others on Julia Street started school at Lincoln Elementary, now Malcolm X. Lincoln was a neighborhood school which meant it was segregated. Nearly all the students at Lincoln were Colored. According to my siblings there were a handful of Mexican and White students, but they don't know where they lived. On our street and on the surrounding streets there were a few Japanese families whose children also attended Lincoln. The two Japanese families on our block owned homes next door to each other. Like so many others, they were interned during the war. When the war ended, they came back to reclaim their homes and their place in the community. We never heard their stories. They were friendly from a distance, they tended to interact only with each other.

Despite almost all the students in South Berkeley being Colored, at the time there was only one Colored teacher in the entire Berkeley Unified School District, Ms. Ruth Acty. Ms. Acty was hired in 1943 at Lincoln where she taught with distinction for years. There were no Colored administrators. The janitor was a Colored man. Separate and unequal education and no representation in the faculty or administration was exactly what my family had left behind in Chicago.

Note

- As of Spring 2021, Emerson Middle School in Berkeley was renamed Ruth Acty Middle School.

BACKGROUND NOISE

EARLY 1950S

I was born in 1953 at Herrick Hospital on Dwight Way in Berkeley, just a few miles from Julia Street where I grew up. Music is my first memory. Our home was filled with the sounds of my mother's favorite recordings from her LP collection; Billie Holiday, Sarah Vaughn, Johnnie Hartman, Ella Fitzgerald, Andy and the Bey Sisters, Morgana King, Ben Webster, Duke Ellington, just to name a few. We were wrapped in music, mostly Jazz, from the time we woke up until we went to sleep. I was comforted by music, I still am.

In our home listening to music was not a passive endeavor. Along with the music came conversation, commentary, and quizzes from my mother. She analyzed the lyrics, the notes, the phrasing, and the silence between the notes. She shared her analysis and tested whoever was in the room, regularly. It was all in good fun, but she was serious about it. To this day whenever I hear one of her favorite songs, and she had many, I search my brain, as if readying for the test, until I find the details she shared so freely. I am comforted by the ritual because it reminds me of her. This early training and our family culture created my love of music, words, and the sound of words and when strung together, their cadence.

There was always a steady stream of visitors at our house on Julia Street. Most came with music choices in hand ready to share their new discoveries, or intent on hearing my mother's latest records. It was so constant it was almost background noise. I learned to tune it all in or out depending on necessity. Music and the accompanying soundtrack of a good time were constants. I found it comforting. I still do.

By the time I was five years old, my siblings were teenagers; nineteen, eighteen, fifteen, and thirteen. From my vantage point they were the most wondrous people in the world. Still are. From my vantage point it seemed they and their friends were living in a wonderland where only teens were welcome. Whenever they gathered at our home, which was often, I sat quietly on the outer edge of the living room listening to their stories, silently inserting myself into the action, making their stories my own. Whenever someone said, "remember when" I would silently reply "I remember." At least in my mind I was a member of the group.

Only when the teens were not convened in our living room did I go out to create memories of my own. My first friendships with kids my own age were kids who lived within a short walking distance, a few houses down or right across the street. Although we were only five years old, we had free reign of the neighborhood. We spent our days and evenings going in and out of each other's homes creating adventures that bring a smile to this day; sleep-overs, writing plays which we performed for passersby from my friend's balcony, being pests to our older siblings. With my fertile imagination I began committing my siblings' stories to memory, comingling their stories with my own creating a place that was the best of both worlds.

Either I didn't notice, or I didn't have the tools to process what I noticed, but at that time my parents' marriage was faltering. I didn't notice that the regular get-togethers in our home didn't include my father. It didn't register that most evenings he went out. I didn't under-stand the significance, that as he stood with the bathroom door slightly ajar, whistling as he shaved, he was preparing to leave, permanently. I didn't notice that my parents were rarely in the room at the same time. Or when they were, there was little conversation between them, when they spoke it was only to disagree. At the time it didn't register with me that song lyrics had replaced conversation and music filled the silence between them.

Years later when I asked my siblings what our parents were like as a couple before I was born, my oldest sister shared one of her memories. When she was a little girl, they often sat together, the two of them drinking coffee, chatting while reading the newspaper. By the time I came along they were all talked out, they had had their fill of coffee and there was nothing new in the news. My siblings also told me both of our parents had beautiful singing voices, but I never heard either of them sing. By the time I came along there was nothing left to sing about.

Late 1950s

In the fall of 1958 like my siblings before me, I started school at Lincoln Elementary school located just a few blocks from home. As a kindergartner, each day kids from Julia Street walked to school together in a small group escorted by one of the neighborhood moms. She also picked us up after school and took care of us until our parents got home from work. I have very few memories of my time at Lincoln, but I remember some things about kindergarten fondly. It was just a few hours a day and we went either in the morning, designated "Early Birds," or in the afternoon as "Late Birds." I can't remember which group I was in, but I remember while we there we had orange juice and graham crackers and before it was time to go home, we laid down on our mats and took a nap.

Once we were out of kindergarten and into the higher grades, we began to walk the few blocks to and from school in a small unsupervised group. Every morning we walked past Miss Bell's house where she stood on her porch to greet us and wish us a good day at school. We looked forward to seeing her each day and sincerely wished her a good day in return. Miss Bell, a best friend of my grandmother had no children of her own.

Just across the street from Miss Bell's house was a small mom and pop grocery store owned by a Chinese family who lived upstairs from the store. We stopped there every morning to get our supply of penny candy for the day. If the store wasn't open we knocked on the door and someone came downstairs and let us in. As we continued our walk, once we arrived at the busy intersection at the corner of King and Ashby, the Traffic Boys, dressed in their matching sweaters and caps, escorted us safely across the street before we made our way onto the school playground. The Traffic Boys were on duty half an hour before the first bell rang in the morning and as late as half an hour after the last bell rang in the afternoon. They were at their posts rain or shine. On our short walk to and from school we were well taken care of. It never occurred to me, or perhaps to any of us, to be thankful for the kindness shown us each day along the way. It mattered.

As far back as I can remember, for the first few years, the same kids were in my class. At the time I didn't know it but as early as first grade the makeup of our classes was determined by a tracking system intended to separate the slower and faster learners. To draw even more of a distinction there was a "high and low" designation within each grade level. When we started each grade in the fall, we began the year in "low" and after Christmas, if we made normal progress, we were promoted to "high." Movement between low and high was determined by performance and maturity. Both systems, tracking and high/low, were eliminated during my early schooling. Tracking was determined to be discriminatory. I don't know why the high/low designation was started or why it ended.

At Lincoln we were a homogenous group, all from surrounding neighborhoods, from similar economic backgrounds, and we were all Colored. Because we were all Colored, race was not an issue we dealt with at school. But racism was insidious and always lurking under the surface. It was only spoken about at home and in our community. At home, I overheard my parents or siblings talk about things that were probably not intended for me to hear. Or maybe they were for me to hear, by way of preparation. Among themselves they shared events of the day, often funny, usually benign, but there were incidents that they felt were unfair, out of order or were just mean. There were times when they felt they'd been singled out, treated poorly, or left out because of their race. They never groused or even complained, their stories were told with a weariness that indicated a tacit acceptance but never defeat. When they told their stories, the rejoinder was typically "that's just the way it is." But they always looked for a workaround, a way to mitigate situations that were inherently not in their favor. They looked for ways to make things work. Sometimes it got to be too much, and they had their own way of dealing. About work issues my father always said, "you can't pick your relatives, but you can pick your employers." I assume if it got to be too much at work, he exercised his right to pick his employer. When things were too much my mother had her way of letting her displeasure be known. I remember one Saturday when I was quite young, we had gone to San Francisco to shop for back-to-school clothes. For fun window shopping, we went into one of the fancier stores, when we walked in every saleswoman stopped what she was doing and stared at us. I remember taking my mother's hand and whispering, "Why are they staring?" My mother replied in a voice that was intended to carry, "They're staring at us because we're gorgeous." She then swept over to the perfume counter where she liberally sprayed herself and me with My Sin, her favorite scent, and then she swept, with me in tow, out of the store. Almost more than the details of the incident, I remember how I felt. At the same time, I felt shame and pride. Ashamed that maybe we didn't fit in and proud of my mother's response. Almost sixty years later I remember how I felt that day.

When they told their stories, the pain was palpable. I will likely never forget the stories of how my oldest brothers were treated, on two separate occasions. One incident illustrates the covert ways in which race is used as a weapon and the other incident is much more overt. Just after high school graduation my oldest brother took the test to work at the Berkeley post office to earn money for college. He received a letter informing him he had passed the test and was given a time to report for an interview. In anticipation, he got there early, gave the door monitor (who was White) his name. The man began looking for my brother's name, starting half-way down the list. Looking at the list twice, each time starting from the middle, and looking down to the bottom, he declared "your name's not here." My brother asked if he could "take a look." He found his name at the top of the page. The list was in order of highest score to lowest. My brother's score was the highest. This happened in 1957, I was four years old, perhaps the first time I heard this story.

They had walked straight down California Street, a quiet two-lane street with family homes lining each side. They had only walked a few blocks when they noticed a police car keeping pace with them, when suddenly the car stopped, and a policeman got out. He rushed over and asked the girl what she was doing in "that" neighborhood.

You see, she was White and my brother, Colored. And they were in South Berkeley, the all-Colored part of town. All-Colored by design. The blue-eyed teenaged blonde girl responded incredulously that she was going to visit with her friend in his home. The officer gave her one last chance to say she was not alright. She said she was fine, and he got back in his car. That wasn't the end of it. In his police car, the officer drove slowly along-side them until they got to our house. After a short visit, my brother walked his friend back to campus. When he got back home my mother gently told him, "You know you can't bring that girl back here." He replied sadly, "I know." That happened in 1958 in harmonious, liberal, redlined, segregated by design, Berkeley. I was five years old.

STATUS CHANGE
1960-1962

In 1960 my little brother was born and evened the scales again, three girls and three boys. My mother referred to us as "the first four, then Tina, then Tony" (because the first four were born one right after the other and then me eight years later and then Tony nearly eight years after me). Or she called us her "half dozen long stemmed roses." Either way we were a perfectly matched set. The moment my little brother was born my status changed. I was no longer the youngest. I had lost my place in line, but on sight I fell in love with him. I still am.

Shortly after my little brother was born my father moved out of the house, but he didn't move far away. Over the next few years one by one my older siblings got married and started families of their own. In short order, in my home, I went from being the youngest of five siblings to being the oldest of two. I was not yet eight years old, and it was a lot of change in a short period. I did not do well with the changes. Adults say children are resilient. I say adults say that to make themselves feel better. I say kids just don't know any better. They don't have a frame of reference, no yardstick, no way to make comparisons. At eight years old I could not fully understand or articulate my feelings, but I remember that it felt like a lot to deal with. My mother must have noticed my unease because on my eighth birthday I got home from school just in time to hear the KJAZ deejay make a dedication to me from my mother. She had asked him to play "I'm Glad There is You," sung by Sarah Vaughn. Some of the lyrics are "In this world of ordinary people, extraordinary people, I'm glad there is you. In this world of overrated pleasures and underrated treasures, I'm glad there is you." At that moment, the world, and my place in it were clear.

Despite the many changes, some things never changed, my love for my family in any iteration, the prevalence of music in our lives and the regularity of visitors in our home. Over the years my siblings and their families joined the steady stream of regular visitors. I found them comforting. I still do.

My neighborhood was changing too. At first the differences were subtle and not nearly as impactful as the changes happening within my own home. Dear friends who were neighbors moved away and several single-family homes were converted into multi-family units. The makeup of the families within the units began to change; there were more single parent households. People were more inwardly focused, perhaps stretched too thin to be mindful of other people's children. Some of the original homeowners regarded some of the renters as different or as less than, judging rather than embracing their children. The village was becoming less of a village.

Sacramento Street the major thoroughfare which was home to the much-frequented Colored owned and operated businesses was undergoing a transformation; businesses were closing, changing ownership, or relocating outside of the neighborhood. The pool hall, liquor store, and tiny night club which had sat side by side in the shadows for years took on more prominence. Men who had once been content to spend their time inside of those shadow establishments began to loiter in front. On occasion my father could be seen among them.

Where we were once used to visiting the family grocer next door to the pool hall without a care, we became increasingly more cautious about our surroundings. Police actions which were largely unheard of in the area were becoming more commonplace. Little by little, the tone and tenor of our harmonious, homogeneous all-Colored working-class neighborhood, like so many things, was not what it once was.

In third grade I was transferred from Lincoln Elementary to Longfellow Elementary, equal distance from my home but in the opposite direction. This change on its face was minor, but on closer inspection it meant there was no one to wish us well every morning on the way to school. It was another loss. It mattered.

When I was transferred to Longfellow, now a middle school, I also skipped a grade. No one explained the reason I changed schools or why I was put in a higher grade. Like most kids at that time, I did what I was told without question or discussion. Years later I learned the district lines had been changed, requiring students on one side of Julia Street to continue at Lincoln and on the other side, my side, to attend Longfellow. Like Lincoln, Longfellow was a neighborhood school which meant that nearly one hundred percent of the student body was Colored. Unlike Lincoln, where there was just one big campus housing everyone, at Longfellow kindergarteners were housed in bungalows across the street from the main campus. Inside their fenced yard right outside of the bungalows the kindergarteners had their own little playground. There was no need for a cafeteria as the kindergartners were at home during lunchtime. Older kids were forbidden to go across the street into the kindergarten area without a pass from the office. The kindergarten students were not allowed to cross the street to the larger campus under any circumstances. The main campus where the students in the higher grades were housed had two playgrounds. The Big Side playground was for students in grades four, five, and six and the Little Side playground for students in grades one, two, and three. The two playgrounds were separated by the main building which held the administrative offices and most of the classrooms. Sprinkled around the main building were small portable buildings which were added or taken away as the student population changed.

Longfellow is where I made friends with kids who had not attended Lincoln or did not live in the 1500 block of Julia Street. Some are still my friends. At Longfellow, like at Lincoln, almost all of us lived in surrounding neighborhoods and were more alike than different. But there were differences. It was at that time that I noticed there were kids in my class who were not exactly like me. There were kids who came from different backgrounds, had a different upbringing. An example is my friend Susan. For a reason that I can't remember, for at least one full school year, rather than walk to school with kids on my street I walked to school with Susan, a girl who did not live in my neighborhood. I don't even remember how we met. I don't know where she lived, exactly. I know she lived south of Ashby Avenue and each morning we met on the corner of Julia and Sacramento Streets and walked together for five blocks. We parted ways at Longfellow where I went into the building, and she continued along Sacramento Street. All these years later I assume she attended the all-girls Catholic School which I didn't even know existed back then. My memory of her is vague but I remember she was different. I found it odd that although she was my age, lived in the area and was Colored, she didn't attend Longfellow or Lincoln. I found it odd that she didn't dress like me and the other girls my age. She wore the same thing every day, a cardigan sweater, white blouse, plaid pleated skirt, white knee-high socks and white saddle oxford shoes, which I later learned was her official school uniform. She wore her hair curled with ribbons, not in the plaits we all wore. Many of the details of her appearance were different and were meticulously attended to. While I remember everything about the way she looked, I remember nothing about who she was. I'm sure that says something about me. Although her existence in my life was brief and my memories of her shallow, I mention this only because I am sure knowing her broadened my perspective. I never saw her again after that school year.

At that time, life should have been simple. Of course, I had personal worries which on balance were minor, but I had big worries about things that were completely out of my control, like my parents' faltering marriage. Beyond our family problems, my biggest worries were about things I was told to worry about. As a group, at school we regularly worried about earthquakes, polio, and Communism. As a family, by inference, we worried about racism. To combat polio, we were immunized before our parents could enroll us in school. No shots, no school. To be prepared in case of an earthquake, randomly while at school we had earthquake drills. During the drills we all got under our desks, theoretically to shield us in case the building collapsed. Periodically, while at school we were shown clips about the evils of Communism. Maybe as an attempt to ward off the threat of Communism, every morning we stood beside our desks, placed our right hands over our hearts and pledged allegiance to the flag. We did what we were told. We didn't quibble or complain about any of the things. We were told all these things were for our "own good" and we believed it. We took our shots, worried about Communism, and ducked and covered. It was at that time I realized that oddly, there were no drills, newsreels, or pledges to combat or prepare for racism. I was ten years old.

DISCERNMENT
1963

Until sixth grade our group of girlfriends had stood the test of time. Many of us had known each other from the neighborhood even before we started school and others had joined our group during each school year. We were a tight, homogenous, harmonious group. During sixth grade something changed. We began to develop discernment, personal values, and traits we would take with us into adulthood. Just like that our harmonious, homogenous group was not so homogenous or harmonious anymore. Genetic traits and appearance became a major focus. Adjectives were assigned; the girl with the long, wavy hair was known as the girl with "good hair," the boy with light colored eyes was known as the boy with the "pretty eyes," and those with darker skin were called "black' with the intent to demean. We formed cliques; including or excluding each other based on passing whims. More times than not the whims disappeared, and our group was restored but not without hurt feelings, some that never healed.

Until we got to sixth grade almost all the girls at Longfellow wore dresses with little white collars paired with a matching cardigan sweater, white socks, and black and white saddle oxford shoes. For the most part we were content to wear what everyone else wore. The only exception was picture day when girls and boys wore their Sunday best and girls even wore their dress-up hairstyles. Pictures were taken in the morning before the first recess, afterward our outfits were askew, and our hair was no longer picture perfect.

Later in the school year some girls began expressing their individuality through their clothing. Most stuck with some version of "the uniform" throughout sixth grade, eliminating the barrettes from our hair or replacing ankle socks with knee highs. But there were three girls who replaced the entire uniform and because of their choices were earmarked as being "fast." Instead of plaits in their hair they had grown-up hairstyles, wore small hoop earrings in their pierced ears, short skirts, black leather jackets and black leather knee high boots with high heels. Even then I knew their boots would take them places I would never go. There was also a girl, one of the "pretty girls with good hair" who, in sixth grade, stopped coming to school. Rumor was she became hooked on drugs and was led into prostitution. On rare sightings over the years her appearance gave credence to the rumors. The three girls called "fast," which stuck throughout high school, and the girl who stopped coming to school broadened my perspective and helped me create my personal style and boundaries. I am saddened that my growth came at the expense of their own.

In sixth grade real life intruded on my reality, sometimes in a good way. Based on what we saw and heard, we began to develop empathy and concern for people who were not family or close friends. Drawing on our newfound empathy, my sixth-grade teacher, my first male teacher who happened to be Asian, made those of us who understood a concept responsible for helping those who had not caught on. The system was simple and most of the time it worked. We studied in twos, usually a girl and a boy. Usually, the girl was the helper, and the boy was the one being helped. Even then I noticed that the boys who needed the most help were the most disruptive in class. I also noticed and was saddened to note there were a few boys who were quiet and didn't accept help. It seemed they had given up.

It was also in sixth grade that I realized not every student had the benefit of caring adults who lived with them. Some kids did not have clean clothes, money to buy a hot lunch, or a lunch brought from home. There were kids who said bad words, got into fights and talked back to the teacher. I wondered if their circumstances contributed to their behavior. I began to understand cause and effect.

I have always been thoughtful – not always thoughtful in terms of being kind, but thoughtful in terms of thinking things through. At ten years old I thought about the fact that at the age of ten, girls were earmarked as "fast" because of the clothes they wore. At the age of ten, boys were earmarked as "thugs or hoodlums" because of language they used and the way they sometimes behaved. And at the age of ten there were kids who were earmarked as someone who "just didn't fit in." I know now, for the most part, those earmarks stuck.

In sixth grade I learned firsthand there are bullies in the world. There are people who enjoy tormenting, humiliating and victimizing others for their amusement. And there are those who are accomplices or at least they are enablers who stand by laughing and taunting. But there are also kids who, in the face that type of cruelty, are incredibly kind and comforting while putting themselves in the bully's crosshairs. I was bullied for the first and last time during sixth grade. A girl I didn't know made fun of me. She was relentless and cruel. She made recess and lunchtime a sad time for me. One afternoon, I decided I had had enough of her meanness, and we had a fistfight during recess. I started the fight. It was stopped by the woman doing yard duty. I don't know that either of us "won" the fight, but the bullying and teasing stopped. That experience taught me that some people only respond to violence. I also learned I had the capacity to be violent. I never had another fistfight. I learned to use my words. Maybe it was coincidental but at the same time I saw that there was a raw meanness in some kids. They were the ones who put all their might into hitting their opponent with the tetherball or aimed at someone's head when we played dodge ball, intentionally tripped kids as they walked down the hall, or pulled the chair away as someone sat down. They tried to write their meanness off as pranks but often their pranks became more cruel and vicious overtime. Eventually those who crossed the administration's arbitrary line were dealt with by the system. They were usually expelled. Depending upon where life took them, some I saw again years later in school and some I saw years later loitering on street corners or standing outside of the pool hall.

In spring of 1963, in our last few months at Longfellow, we began to push back on the rules we had been taught to live by. We relaxed our personal dress codes and started to express our individuality. Every day after school rather than going straight home as we had been told, my friends and I took our time and meandered. We were older, our parents were at work, and we were totally in charge of ourselves. Our choices were mostly good, but they were not always the best.

For years we had walked the same route down California Street unbothered until one afternoon a man standing on his front porch asked us if we would like to come in to see his fish tanks. Though we knew better, we jumped at the idea. Once inside we found the fish were plentiful and beautiful. We looked to our hearts content, thanked him, and left. Several days later he asked if we would like to come in and have homemade cookies. Emboldened by our last visit, of course we said yes. We went in, had cookies, thanked him, and left. The following week as we were passing by, he was standing on the walkway at the bottom of his porch with a handful of half dollars. Walking toward us he offered them in exchange for us coming inside. Somehow money changed the game. Somehow, we knew it was a quid pro quo. Somehow instinctively we knew this time it was a bad idea. We refused the offer and ran home. We never talked about it, but we never walked home down California Street again. During that year, for so many reasons, my perception of my little world and my place in it began to change, but it was forever changed in that afternoon. I was ten years old.

Notes

- In 1960 when I was seven, Ruby Bridges, a six-year-old girl, the victim of unbridled hate, had to be escorted to school by United States marshals every morning. The marshals protected her from jeering crowds of adults who assembled along her route. They called her vile names. They spat at her. Her only crime was being enrolled in school while being Colored. People who did not even know her hated her for being Colored. They hated her for being the first Colored student in Louisiana to enroll in a "White" school which, according to law, had been deseg-regated ten years earlier. By the time I was eight years old I became aware of Emmett Till. Although his lynching happened a few years earlier it was a story that was retold, no doubt due to the sheer horror of it. In our home, not often, but over the years if friends requested it, my mother played the Billie Holiday recording "Strange Fruit." The lyrics and Ms. Holiday's rendition of the song painfully expressed the whole culture built up around lynching. It was horrific and it was real. The reality is that on bright sunny afternoons wives/mothers packed picnic lunches while their husbands readied the car so they could spend an afternoon socializing and taking pictures at a lynching. Most times, a Colored male who had been beaten beyond recognition was the victim of their entertainment. It is a horror that can only be characterized as evil. It is a level of hate that is unmatched. Knowing that kind of hatred existed, the world outside of my home and neighborhood seemed less welcoming with every passing year. Knowing that kind of hatred existed, one year never fully prepared me for the next, one hateful event never prepared me for the next. There is no way to prepare. On cue, 1963 brought a familiar brand of evil but on a higher level, built on hate sown in previous years. There was a seemingly endless cavalcade of hate where each act was more horrific than the others.

We had just gone back to school after summer vacation, the start of sixth grade, when on September 15th a bomb was detonated during service at a Colored church in Birmingham, Alabama. Congregants were injured and four little girls were killed. Four girls, my age whose only mistake was being born Colored were murdered while attending a church service. George Wallace the new Governor of Alabama did not rebuke this act of senseless violence, he put a fine point on it. In his inauguration speech the self-proclaimed racist declared his belief in "segregation today, segregation tomorrow, and segregation forever." On that day he proudly captured the attention of the country and perhaps the world with his hate. To ensure his place in history as a racist, on his orders, state troopers armed with mace, pepper spray, and attack dogs were set upon peaceful marchers as they crossed the bridge into Selma in support of Black voter registration. A peaceful protest. There was no shortage of hate in 1963, there was plenty to go around, and not all reserved for Colored people. On a quiet afternoon just a week before our Thanksgiving break, with sadness in his eyes our teacher told us President Kennedy had been shot. I don't remember how our teacher got the news nor do I remember exactly what he said. But I remember his face. His sadness and disbelief were mirrored by every student in our classroom. It was as if someone we knew, a family member or friend, had been shot. I cannot remember how we later learned President Kennedy had died, but when we knew, to a person, even the toughest boys and most aloof girls cried. President Kennedy's assassination was the end of our collective illusions. In our sixth-grade class-room, for us at the age of ten, it was confirmed that evil was real and there were no newsreels, drills, or pledges to combat or prepare for it.

- "We must be concerned not merely about who murdered them, but about the system, the way of life, the philos-ophy that produced the murderer." Dr. Martin Luther King, on the senseless murder of four little girls.

- Home, family, and community are our antidote for hate. The recipe has always been simple and has no doubt provided respite for Colored people forever. When the world is particularly cruel, we draw inward. We look to family, friends, and our community for solace. For as long as I can remember, people from all walks of life, at any time of the day or night were welcome in our home. My mother never turned anyone away and in turn we were always welcomed by friends and neighbors in their homes. With no notice, meals were stretched, drinks were served, and records were put on the turn table. For our family, music was the great leveler, the only calling card needed. Every situation whether it was happy or sad included music.

In September of 1963, the Monterey Jazz Festival made its debut. The festival provided the perfect context for almost everything my mother valued, family, friends, music, food, and drinks. And my mother made sure we were there. The Jazz Festival experience started months in advance when the decision was made that she and her group were going. Whenever they got together, they talked about the lineup and the performers they were most excited to see, they confirmed who was planning to go, their plans for accommodations, and how and when we would get there. The festival lived up to the hype and excitement, but the experience was much more than the venue and performances. Many of the fundamental values that informed our family culture were on view during that weekend, love of family, friends, fellowship, music, good food, and inclusion. During that weekend no one was a stranger. Goodwill was plentiful. The yearly festival became a family tradition.

The flip side of the Jazz Festival, also an extension of our community, was church. We were members of Bethlehem Lutheran Church on Myrtle Street in Oakland. In the middle of the hood in Oakland was this small Lutheran church with a White pastor. The congregants were Colored. We went to church every Sunday morning,

sat quietly while Pastor Cline delivered his quiet,
impactful sermon and were soothed by the quiet hymns.
My favorite parts of the service were the soft hum of my
father sleeping (when he attended) and the end of the
service when Pastor Cline walked down the center aisle
delivering the benediction – "may the Lord bless you and
keep you, may He turn His face toward you and give you
His peace." Pastor Cline met us at the door, shook our
hands and prayed for each of us. He also made house
calls. He was one of us.

It was about that same time that I understood the
importance of our neighborhood and our shared Colored-
ness. The family doctor, pharmacist, cleaners, shoe repair,
hairdresser, charm school, Tots and Teens boutique,
family grocer, milliner, café, all the business owners and
our neighbors, were Colored and important. I thought I
understood what my mother meant when she said, "We
have everything we need here. We don't ever have to leave
the neighborhood." But what I did not fully understand is
that she was simply putting the best face on a difficult
reality. It's what mothers do. When your child isn't invited
to the birthday party, you have a party of your own. In our
neighborhood in South Berkeley, we had a party of our
own. There was a neighborhood milliner because in the
downtown department stores, we were not permitted to
try on hats before we purchased them. Nor could they be
returned if they didn't work out. We had our own hairdressers because White hairdressers could not be both-
ered to learn how to do our hair, nor were we welcome in
their salons. There was a charm school on almost every
corner because I suppose we thought if we adopted their

manners and mannerisms, despite facts in evidence to the contrary, they might like us.

For reasons I can only imagine, I signed myself up for the Etiquette class at the charm school at San Pablo Park. I was about ten years old.

OUT OF OUR COMFORT ZONE
1964

Our seventh-grade class was the first integrated class at Garfield Junior High, now King Middle School. Without fanfare or discussion before or after we started at King, every Monday through Friday morning for two years, my friends and I took the #88 bus from our neighborhood at Ashby and Sacramento, straight up Sacramento Street to Rose Street, beyond University Avenue to Garfield Junior High. Just two miles from home, our destination was an area where many of us had never been before. I don't remember being worried, unhappy, or feeling anything at all about going to an integrated school. I remember I was perturbed at having to spend money on bus fare to get to school every day. Unlike Lincoln and Longfellow, Garfield was too far to walk in the morning and get there on time. With no time limitations in the afternoon, we walked home and spent our bus fare on other things.

Garfield was located on Rose just a couple blocks from Sacramento Street, away from our stomping grounds and out of our comfort zone. I don't remember, maybe we were told, surmised, or imagined that people who lived near the school had concerns about us coming into their neighborhoods. Maybe we had our own concerns about leaving our neighborhood and going into theirs. If there were concerns, they were unwarranted. Where we got off the bus, we were so close to the school we had no need to venture into the surrounding areas. As a result, home-owners who lived near the school had no reason to worry about us and we had no reason to worry about them. Most of us arrived at school after most of them had gone to work and most of us left the area before most of them got back home. I imagine we were as anxious as they were for us to get back to areas where we were familiar.

My overall experience at Garfield was not memorable. I do remember that Garfield felt different, neither good nor bad, just an awareness that we were sharing spaces with people who were not Colored. Before attending Garfield my exposure to White people had been limited to those who were on television, in movies, in magazines, or those who provided a specific service like our pastor, teachers or cashiers at downtown department stores. For the first time I was in class with kids who were not Colored. They were students just like me. Looking back, I am certain many of the White kids in my classes must have been in the same situation. It is likely that for the first time they were with Colored people who were not performing a specific function. We were not domestic day workers, handymen, characters in a television show, a movie or pictured in a magazine. We were all just people.

My observations from my time at Garfield are clouded by the passing of many years and were made by a self-focused seventh or eighth grader. I must have been curious about and maybe a bit leery of my new class-mates. I must have noticed our similarities and our obvious differences. There must have been an undeniable sameness, we were kids about the same age, almost all from Berkeley and all had the prerequisites to sit side by side in a classroom.

Because of my affinity for and love of words, I paid attention to what people said and how they said it. During class discussions I noticed that White students and the teachers had a common baseline of information. On most topics they "spoke the same language." They also seemed to have similar life experiences. But it worked out. If there were issues, we found ways to mitigate, create workarounds, discover commonality, played to our strengths.

To my eye they had their brand of beauty and we had ours. Both groups of kids were comfortable with their own unique gifts, as comfortable as junior high school kids can be. There was little overlap in our God-given looks or our culture-driven styles, therefore no comparisons were made. My friends and I spent none of our time wishing to look or be like them. And as far as I could know they were not comparing themselves to or wishing to be like us either. There were a few girls who tried to appropriate the look of the other culture, but we wrote them off as "trying to be White" or them "trying to be like us." I have very few memories of boys of either race from junior high school. At that point boys were not on my radar.

My memories of my time at Garfield are random and

superficial, focused mostly on appearance. Lots of the White kids had braces on their teeth, something I had not seen much of before. Glasses, braces, hairstyles, and clothes set them apart from us. Our styles were different. My friends and I had "school" clothes and "school" shoes; a set of clothes and shoes that were bought just before school started in the fall intended to last through the entire school year. As the weather dictated, we added a sweater, jacket, or coat based on how cold it got during the fall and winter months. In contrast I remember many of the White kids had what I later learned was "seasonal" clothing; wool sweaters, corduroy jumpers and skirts, tights, long-sleeved button-down blouses, all were put away when the weather changed. In the warmer months, the girls' fall/winter wardrobe was replaced by short-sleeved or sleeveless tops and dresses made of 100% cotton or linen. I can't be sure, but it seemed the clothes they wore were not available where we shopped or maybe we overlooked them. The locations where we shopped were different too. Among themselves some White girls talked about shopping in boutiques near Cal campus or shopping while traveling. My friends and I shopped downtown Berkeley, Oakland, and at El Cerrito Plaza. On special occasions we went to The City, San Francisco, to shop. We also shopped within a common price range, at certain stores. Some of our favorites were JC Penney, Capwell's and Emporium.

Years later I learned about "disposable income" and "life-styles" and "generational debt or wealth" and how those factors varied between ethnic groups and from one family to another. At the time I may not have known what to call it, but at eleven years old I started to recognize the disparity.

Notes

   - Although we sat side by side in the classroom, outside of the classroom we did our thing, and they did theirs. Even in my second year at Garfield, I am not proud to say that none of the White students in my classes were part of my circle. To an extent it was as if they were not there. It is not that I was unkind to them or them to me; we just did not exist to each other outside of sharing space in a classroom. I had my circle of friends and they had theirs. Some kids mixed between groups and some students developed friendships with kids outside of their race. My circle of friends grew at Garfield, but only by including new Colored friends.

   - I had my first Colored teacher at Garfield in seventh grade. Miss Barbara Cannon was my Glee teacher. She is serendipitously, coincidentally the first cousin of the man I met and married years later. On that note, Garfield was a net positive.

   - Brought up in the Lutheran church, when I was eleven my mother enrolled me in Catechism class. It was two hours every Saturday afternoon, noon to 2pm. It lasted for months. To say that it seriously negatively impacted my social life seems wrong since it was religious studies. But it seriously negatively impacted my social life. Saturday was the day that friends got together to go shopping and have fun. Spending an hour on the bus each way and then two hours in class every Saturday for months, did not make me happy. Mostly I was afraid I would miss out by not being in the mix. No amount of whining and complaining changed my mother's mind. Despite being easygoing most of the time, once she had made up her mind, she rarely changed her decision. I went to Catechism class every Saturday and I was confirmed with the others in my class, right on schedule. I learned where to find life affirming scriptures that I still call on to sustain me. More important, at eleven years old, I learned despite my being convinced it won't, life does go on.

- Fall of 1965, my little brother started school at Longfellow Elementary. By then, just two years after Berkeley desegregated the schools, Longfellow was no longer a neighborhood school. Kids were bused from all over Berkeley to attend. It was at Longfellow that he met his wife who was one of the kids who was bused in. Net positive.

- Because hate is always waiting in the wings, in August 1965, just before we started eighth grade, a Black man was stopped for a traffic violation in Watts. The stop turned deadly. As a result of how people felt the driver was treated, the incident triggered days of protests and riots. Thirty-four people were killed and neighborhoods in Watts and surrounding areas were left in ruin. I remember watching as the story unfolded on television, news clip after news clip and update after update. Each update was more inconceivable than the last. We talked about it at home and among our friends, but I don't remember any discussion of the events in any of my classes at school. Facilitated discussions at school might have helped or at least signaled that someone outside of our community cared. I could not understand how a single traffic stop could lead to thirty-four people being dead, one thousand people injured, and untold property being destroyed. Over fifty years later the aftermath of those six days of rioting still lingers. At twelve, I had a hard time with it. Fifty-six years later I still do.

WE WERE IN A BUBBLE
1966 -1967

Every ninth-grade student in Berkeley who didn't attend private school went to West Campus formerly named Burbank. And it was great. Of course, at the time we didn't know it, but that year was as close to perfect as a school year could be. We were too old for babysitters and too young to get into any real trouble. We were in a bubble. We were a homogeneous group within a bubble. We were the same age, had similar educational experiences, similar backgrounds and almost all were from Berkeley. By then, after two years in junior high, most had reconciled any differences. There seemed to be tacit agreement that, yes in theory we were at West Campus to learn, but for the most part we wanted to have fun. We wanted to have preliminary fun in preparation for the real fun we knew we were going to have when we got to Berkeley High.

Despite shared goals and our sameness, it was our differences that made the year at West Campus enlightening and encouraged a broadening of perspectives.

Accustomed to the differences attributed to race, we became more aware of class distinctions and cultural anomalies. We began to understand that cultural differences were not just limited to those attributed to ethnic groups, but there were cultural differences from one religion to another, one neighborhood to another, one family to the next. During that year, we began to embrace ourselves as fully as we embraced others. We recognized that family culture is foundational to who we are and how we show up in the world. On the surface we may have been a homogenous group, but we were complex in our individual uniqueness.

We came from all corners of Berkeley. Some came from the flats, some came from the waterfront, and some came from the East hills. We were proud of where we came from. In my opinion, the luckiest among us came from my neighborhood in redlined, segregated by design, South Berkeley. Within South Berkeley, and other similar areas, we came from neighborhoods where we were fortunate enough to be able to look to our own family or to the family next door or across the street for examples of excellence.

I assume almost everyone, regardless of what part of Berkeley they came from felt they were the lucky ones. I assume most felt their neighborhood was a great place to live and most of the people in their neighborhood were extraordinary. But time after time, by any measure my neighborhood, at least in my mind, was firmly at the top of any goodness list. My assessment proved correct daily, I was able to get most anything I needed from a neighborhood business, just steps from my home, owned by a neighbor who happened to be Black.

Notes

- Our neighborhood and its specialness were highlighted spectacularly in October of 1966 when one of the freight trains which ran twice a day down the tracks in the median on Sacramento Street, made a once in a lifetime stop on the corner of Julia Street (my street!) at Sacramento. That afternoon the train was carrying then presidential candidate Bobby Kennedy and entourage on route to a campaign rally at UC Berkeley. To my knowledge no one in the neighborhood knew they were coming. The crowd grew organically and joyously. I can't remember exactly what Mr. Kennedy said but I remember how I felt. I was elated, I felt part of something much bigger and I was proud to be exactly where I was standing. Good feelings were contagious. Mr. Kennedy spoke to the crowd, the crowd chanted and cheered in response. It was reminiscent of 'call and response' heard every Sunday morning at most any Black church. He loved us and we loved him back. That day and how I felt on that day are among my most vivid memories. I was elated by and proud of the warm welcome South Berkeley gave Bobby Kennedy. I think of that day fondly and mourn his loss still, over fifty years later. Although Bobby Kennedy's visit momentarily set South Berkeley apart on the world stage, his message told us we were all in the struggle together. In retrospect his message summed up our time as ninth grade students, in our homogenous bubble at West Campus. We were all in it together. Some of us came from "traditional" homes, some from broken families, some came from money, some came from working-class families, and others were subsisting at poverty level, but Monday through Friday, for seven hours a day, our differences didn't matter. For seven hours a day, Monday through Friday, it felt like we rowed in the same direction, making our way to Berkeley High.

- During those years I made some life decisions that I continue to honor. I made the choice not smoke after smoking on the bus on the way to and from school for a week. After that week I decided smoking was too expensive and smelled terrible. I also decided that bad words were not for me, they never seemed to fit. To this day the only bad word I have used is BS, the full version, and only at work when I wanted to emphasize that something was truly BS. My father's drinking made me turn away from alcohol. And the sad stories of those who covertly bought and sold drugs in and around my neighborhood proved more than a cautionary tale. I had seen enough to know that some things were not for me. I was thirteen.

I LOVED HIGH SCHOOL

1967-1968

September 1967, at long last we had made it to Berkeley High. We had sorted out our segregation or integration issues if we had any. We were at least comfortable with or had built friendships with kids from other cultures. We embraced and celebrated our sameness and our differences.

My circle remained unchanged, 100% of my friends were Black, but I was more interested in and friendlier with kids who were not Black. We still didn't spend time with White kids at school outside of class, nor did we visit each other's homes or socialize together. Other Black kids did.

Schoolwork didn't hold my full attention. I was an above average student, but when I found a topic compelling, I excelled. Despite my intermittent interest in the subject matter, I loved high school. I loved being a student at Berkeley High. It was highly regarded for sports, the arts, academics, and it was where the cool kids went. I took full advantage of every social opportunity

Berkeley High had to offer. I went to rallies, dances, club meetings, performances, and sporting events. Socially, I was happy and thrived.

In the evening after school, I was sort of in charge of myself and my little brother. As she had for a while, my mother continued to work on swing shift at the Oakland Army Base. My father lived a few miles away from our family home and was very much in the picture. Being a carpenter in and around the city and having friends in the trades who might see me, my freedom to roam or misbehave was seriously curtailed. So, I pretty much stayed on the straight and narrow. That isn't to say that I didn't have fun or bend the rules. I did.

My first few months at Berkeley High were a continuation of the fun I had while at West Campus but with more freedom. Since my mother was usually sleeping when I left in the morning and at work when I got home my choices were largely my own. We had an open campus at lunchtime. We could eat in the cafeteria which my friends and I rarely did. We could eat outside on campus which we never did. Almost all the time, we chose to eat our lunch downtown Berkeley. There were several places we could afford where the staff didn't bother us if we came in a little before lunchtime and stayed a little after.

For a while there was a teen "night club." It was a place to dance to our favorite songs, have our favorite soft drinks and snacks. Doors opened in the afternoon right after school. It wasn't expensive and we went often. We took full advantage of our freedom. We were on our own, on our honor. We had real fun while we made sure to stay out of any real trouble. Real trouble was anything that required a parent to get involved.

Note

- Because hate was always lurking just beneath the surface, we were braced for the punches when they landed. In April of 1968, Dr. Martin Luther King, Jr. was assassinated in broad daylight. I wondered how something so terrible could happen to a man who was so loved and revered. Even those who disagreed with him respected him for his non-violent approach in his pursuit of social justice. Before we could recover from Dr. King being killed, in June as we were counting down the days until the last day of school, presidential candidate Bobby Kennedy was assassinated. To me he was more than a politician because of his unscheduled stop in South Berkeley on his way to Cal campus. He had ridden the same Santa Fe train that passed through South Berkeley at least twice a day, the same train my older brothers claimed to have ridden to Burbank junior high on occasion. The same train that traveled the route Santa Fe trains had traveled for as long as my family lived on Julia Street. Even now, in my mind, I can hear the faint sound of a train whistle in the still of the late night.

At that point, as a teenager, I was no more able to understand or reconcile the unbridled hatred that led to the assassination of these great men than I was at age four when hate was only an uncomfortable notion. I mourned these men not just from my personal sense of loss but for the loss to our country. With the innocence of youth, I had been certain Dr. King, through love, would stem the tide of hate and Bobby Kennedy would fulfill the promises his brother had made to our community and to our nation. It felt like the end of hope, I was fifteen.

1968 - 1969

In our junior year, my friends and I started our own social club. It was not affiliated with Berkeley High therefore was not regulated by school rules or guidelines. Our club was entirely our own. We elected officers, decided our agenda, had regular meetings, and maintained a full social calendar. We had our meetings at the YMCA located a few blocks from campus. For two years, as a club, we planned fundraisers, sponsored bus trips, and held dances at the local YMCA branches, downtown Berkeley and on California Street in South Berkeley.

Because we were organized, responsible, and stayed out of trouble, adults gave us a wide berth. We navigated on our own unless or until we needed adult intervention. We worked hard to make sure we never needed adult intervention. I can't remember how we partnered with the YMCA, how we got access to meeting rooms or space to hold our dances or how we negotiated contracts without an adult, but we did. I was president of the club for at least a year. It was during those months that I honed skills that I draw on today. Building skills early in life contributed to my sense of where I fit in the world. We had the best of times, and we knew it.

My mother was still working at the Army Base. She

worked 3pm to 11pm Monday through Friday, which meant I would see her in the morning before I left for school and not again until almost midnight. One of my older sisters had moved back home but she had a full-time job in San Francisco and a life of her own which meant I was somewhat in charge of myself and my little brother. I pushed the envelope, doing just enough to have fun but not so much that I caused trouble.

My mother's primary responsibility at the Army Base was getting equipment where it was supposed to be, intact and on time. At that time, she was intimately involved with the underpinnings of the logistics of the Viet Nam War. The war loomed large. Newscasts and newspapers reported the horrors of war and the number of American casualties, multiple times daily.

Berkeley was regularly in the national news; known for its liberal and radical views. That reputation was largely the result of actions of U.C. Berkeley students. There were daily protests on campus, usually on Sproul Plaza, which were reported enthusiastically around the world by the media. Tensions and protests were at a fever pitch when in May of 1969, just as we were counting down the days until summer break, the National Guard was dispatched to Berkeley, taking over the downtown area. As a result of a clash between UC Berkeley administrators and a group of Berkeley residents and students, martial law was declared by President Reagan, a curfew imposed and national guardsmen with unsheathed bayonets and live ammunition occupied our downtown. A military helicopter doused protesters with tear gas. They were protesting the war and were in a battle to keep "People's

Park" as a park for the people rather than to be used as a parking lot for Cal students. We were curious about what was happening, but we only got as close to the action as the barricades and common sense allowed. It was surreal. As teens, the battle for People's Park or protesting the War was not our thing. My friends and I were kids, to us the War was a world away and People's Park was mostly inhabited by White hippies. We didn't go to People's Park. We thought the park was a place for hippies to congregate and use drugs. The War, the park, none of it was our fight.

We were interested in and fascinated by the Black Panthers and Black Muslims. Both groups were embedded in our community, part of the landscape. Both groups were iconic, fueled by the attention they garnered from the media and the duality of their impact on society. No one I knew was an actual member of either organization but many of my friends adopted their style. The Black Muslim men dressed in suits, crisp white shirts, and ties daily. The women wore modest outfits, their hair was covered, their arms and legs were covered, and they wore closed toe shoes. Unless you were a member you had no visibility into the Black Muslim's agenda. All we knew was what we saw and what we imagined.

The Black Panthers were more flamboyant and had a larger-than-life community presence. The women who were the face of the movement, Angela Davis and Kathleen Cleaver were brilliant and beautiful. Huey Newton, co-founder, was handsome and charismatic. They dressed in all black; black beret, black leather jacket, black turtleneck and trousers and carried large black rifles. Their stated primary role was to police the community, to ward off crime and eliminate police brutality. The Black Panthers had a hands-on, measurable positive impact on the Black community despite their portrayal in the media. In addition to their policing role, they created a breakfast program which fed hungry children before sending them off to school and an after-school tutoring program that provided help and supervision for children who would have often gone home to an empty house or become involved in something much worse.

Notes

- That winter was colder than it had ever been in our lifetime. We usually wore miniskirts to school, but to ward off the wind and near freezing temperatures we insisted that we be allowed to wear pants. Ours was the first class of girls to wear pants at Berkeley High School. When the cold snap broke, we kept wearing them.

- As of Summer 2021, People's Park supporters and UC Berkeley administrators are at odds over the land, again or still.

UNDERSERVED
1969

It was summer 1969, the summer before my senior year at Berkeley High. After living my whole life in redlined, segregated by design South Berkeley, that summer I learned that I came from a community that was "underserved." I can't remember the details of how I came to be interviewed and selected for a job sponsored by the Neighborhood Youth Corps, but NYC was a program that sought to level the playing field for "youth from underserved communities." Until I read the collateral included with my official welcome letter, I had no idea that our all Black, working-class neighborhood was considered lacking in any way. For most of my life, on my street, the people who lived in each home were the original owners. With rare exception, each home held a family made up of two parents and at least a couple of kids. With rare exception, both parents had jobs, the kids attended school, yards and homes were well kept and there was no trouble. My next-door neighbors to the left, husband and wife were both teachers. Directly across the street the homeowners also owned a fish market located a few blocks down on Sacramento Street. Another neighbor worked for the School of the Deaf. Many were employed by the government. Within steps of my house, on Sacramento Street there was a family doctor, a pharmacist, jeweler, cleaners, shoe repair, café, creamery, liquor store, variety store, pool hall, mom and pop grocery store, two beauty shops, charm school, and a small night club. All neighborhood businesses were owned and run by Black people who also owned homes in the surrounding neighborhoods. It was from my family and our neighbors that I learned almost everything I knew about everything. How could I possibly be underserved?

It was as if the letter declaring our neighborhood underserved had been prophetic. As if on cue, a steady stream of long-time neighbors began to move away. Black men were being siphoned off into the military to feed the Viet Nam War machine or sentenced to harsh prison terms for relatively minor crimes. When circumstances conspired in the worst possible way mothers were left to raise children on their own. Where there was once a "village" approach to child rearing, the village devolved into "every (wo)man for himself." By the end of that summer my neighborhood had gone through an almost complete transformation. Single family homes were being replaced by apartment buildings. Once beautiful front yards had been paved with concrete, those not concrete were left unattended. Businesses changed owners. Storefronts went without tenants. Drugs infiltrated the area. Menacing men stood outside the pool hall, replacing men who were harmless. Some of the replacements were not yet men.

They were boys, some the same boys who had been disruptive in class or had given up on school in sixth grade. Crime increased alarmingly. There was a constant police presence on the corner of Julia (my street!) and Sacramento streets in the form an actual police bus. The changes in my neighborhood mirrored changes in many neighborhoods that had once been the pride of Black homeowners and Black business owners. My perspective was broadened. Without my consent I became aware of issues and circumstances beyond my own little world, above my pay grade, I was fighting above my weight class. And once you know things, it is impossible to unknow them.

Viet Nam had been "their war" until the time when many of my older male friends and classmates began to weigh their options and realized they didn't have any once they had graduated from high school. Some enlisted; inexplicably they wanted to serve a country where they had been routinely underserved. But most of the young men from the surrounding neighborhoods who went to Viet Nam were drafted. Because many had no plan and no means to go to college, unlike many of their college bound White peers, they were headed to the front lines. By then there were nearly half a million US troops in Viet Nam and twenty three percent were Black. Disproportionate in that Black people made up only eleven percent of the population of the United States. Again, I was aware of disparity.

The war was at its most unpopular. From my Neighborhood Youth Corp job for underserved youth at UC Berkeley, I looked out on Sproul Plaza where students and

Berkeley residents protested the war every day. I was made keenly aware of the war by the daily protests, friends being drafted and my mother's work at the Oakland Army Base.

The war was front and center. The nightly news and newspaper headlines told unflattering tales of an unpopular war. The nightly count of the dead and wounded kept the war top of mind. Almost sadder than the deaths, was the influx of returning soldiers, many with mental and physical injuries that would never heal. They were a constant reminder of the futility of war. Without my consent, I was aware. And once you know, it is impossible to unknow.

Just as I was making my way toward graduation at Berkeley High my mother was accepted into UC Berkeley and she started her journey toward her undergrad and master's degrees while working full time, still on swing shift. My mother rarely shared the intense aspects of her job, but for her the Viet Nam war was always top of mind. It was also rare that she discussed the continuing vestiges of racial discrimination in her workplace, racism that continued despite the passage of the anti-discrimination legislation in 1963. One night, as usual after my mother got home from work several family friends stopped in. As usual they listened to music, made conversation, and had drinks. Most unusual, my mother shared her private thoughts. Something must have happened during her shift at work that spurred her to find and read a letter she had received in response to an application she had submitted for a promotion. The letter said, 'although you are the most qualified, have the highest number of commendations, and excelled on the written and in-person interviews, we will not be offering you the promotion at this time. Instead, we are promoting (they shared the other candidate's name). My mother never suggested the woman got the job because she was White, but there was sadness and weariness in her voice that suggested the woman got the job because she was White. When she told the story that time, I was sixteen.

Notes

- Maybe I should have recognized that ours and the surrounding neighborhoods were woefully underserved. Maybe I should have paid attention to the fact that nowhere in the East hills or adjacent areas would you find train tracks and freight trains trundling through the neighborhood twice a day. Nor would you find a liquor store on every corner, pool halls and night clubs with the requisite men loitering outside, within feet of people's homes. Maybe it should have been of note that there was a bus line that offered service to and from South Berkeley only twice a day; once early in the morning in time to get domestic workers up to the East hills to start their employers' day and came down again only after dinner was served, dishes were done and the home set to rights so that their employer could enjoy the evening.

- During that summer I met and fell for the man I married years later. We're still married and I'm still glad I fell.

COULDN'T NOBODY TELL US NOTHIN
1969 - 1970

We were seniors at Berkeley High and couldn't nobody tell us nothin. Berkeley High, the only public school in town was home to handsome boys and pretty girls. We were the mighty Yellow Jackets. Our sports teams were the best of the best, Black players dominated in most every field, football, track, and basketball. It was the heyday of the Fresno Relays and the Tournament of Champions (TOC – Oakland Coliseum), where Berkeley High was the star of the show. The Berkeley High Jazz Band was well renowned, Theater and the Arts well respected. Berkeley High had a newly created Black Studies Program.

Our Blackness loomed large. We wore our Blackness proudly in our hairstyles, music, and fashions. We wore Blackness as a mantel, in dashikis and African dresses, African jewelry, magnificent afros and elaborately braided hairstyles. We saw Blackness in our communities as the Black Panthers fed school children and Black Muslims fed us bean pie. We heard it in our poetry in the form of spoken word from Gil Scott Heron and Nikki Giovanni.

We danced to it until the wee hours while James Brown demanded that we Say it Loud, I'm Black and I'm proud. We partied hard, but according to the old school definition of "partied," which meant we danced and danced and danced; no drugs, no alcohol, at least not that I am aware of. We danced from the time the party or dance got started until it was time to go home. And there was a party or dance on most every Friday and Saturday night. Senior year was a blur of socializing and making sure we had enough credits to graduate.

And just like that, it was over. It was Graduation Day, Friday June 12, 1970. We, the Berkeley High Class of 1970 gathered front and center at the Greek Theatre, poised to take on the world. The speeches were just "Berkeley" enough, but for our taste not quite brief enough. There were shenanigans, but the administration indulged us as we celebrated the end of our era. At the end of the ceremony, without the aid of cell phones we were able to find family and friends, where we spent the requisite amount of time taking photos and receiving best wishes. Later that evening, after the obligatory family party, the real celebration started. We partied into the night, celebrating our accomplishment and dancing to our favorite records; "Oh What a Night."

And just like that, after a summer to remember it was all over. We scattered; some went away to college, others stayed local, attending Cal Berkeley, Cal State Hayward, Merritt, or Laney. Some got jobs at BART, P.G.&E., the Telephone Company, with the Government, or in the private sector. In some ways our Blackness, through affirmative action programs, provided us opportunities in employment, education, and housing. We were considered and accepted where few Black people had access before. Many Black families boasted the first member to attend college or to secure a position on a career track. While still others found themselves on track to go nowhere.

Notes

- As I prepared for my Senior Ball, finding nothing that I liked in the stores, I planned to have my ensemble made. I'm sure my sense of style had been influenced by the fashions worn by the women in my family and those who frequented our home when I was growing up. One particularly glamorous couple, the Holfords, both were teachers, and they made an indelible mark on me. The only time I saw them was when they stopped by on their way home from a formal affair or cocktail party. Depending upon the occasion Mr. Holford wore a well-fitting dinner jacket or tux while Mrs. Holford was stunning in just below the knee cocktail dresses or floor length gowns made of sumptuous fabrics. Her accessories were understated yet striking. She always wore fur, either a stole, jacket, or full-length mink. When my parents attended similar functions, they too were a very pretty picture.

With fashions from years gone by in mind, I found a seamstress, perfect patterns, and beautiful fabrics. As I was looking for the perfect buttons, the crowning jewels of the outfit, in an unlocked case I saw the most beautiful buttons I couldn't have even imagined. They were multifaceted, they sparkled like jewels. Way out of my price range, they were $2.00 each. I needed eight. It was at that moment that half-truths, little white lies, and justifications showed up. When no one was looking I put eight buttons in my pocket. I had never taken anything before, nor have I since. Afterwards I felt bad for taking them but not bad enough to take them back or not bad enough not to use them. To this day I am not able to call it what it was, stealing. To this day taking the buttons is among the worst decisions I have ever made. That was a pivot point. I have made many other bad decisions, but that one haunts me. I was seventeen. I knew better.

- Life is full of surprises and the world is small. Turns out Mrs. Holford, half of the most glamorous couple I have ever seen, was my husband's second grade teacher. Years ago, his mother reminded him of the crush he had on Mrs. Holford. I guess he found her glamorous too.

THE MATCHED SET WAS BROKEN
1970 - 1974

During the summer, just weeks after my graduation my sister was diagnosed with schizophrenia. Our family never fully recovered. One piece of the matched set of three boys and three girls, was broken. My beautiful, brilliant sister was only twenty-five when the disease robbed her of the life and future that she had worked so hard to secure. At that time mental illness was not talked about, particularly not within our community. My mother spent untold hours attempting to get information and help, but I don't think she ever accepted the diagnosis. We struggled as a family, each of us reacted based upon who we were at the time.

I had just graduated from high school, and I was shell shocked. I didn't have a plan. So, I looked for and found a job. In fall of 1970 I moved out of the house into an apartment with a roommate and enrolled in one local junior college after the other, Merritt, Contra Costa, Grove Street and Laney. For a while I worked at a men's clothing store downtown Oakland where on the weekend men would shop with their wives but on Monday, they came back to ask me out. While working there I learned a lot about what some men thought of women and what they thought was our place in the world. I also saw drug addiction up close as every day well-known drug addicts came into the store to steal to support their daily drug habit. This was before the Crack Epidemic devastated Black communities and as bad as it was, it only got worse. As the areas I walked through to get to and from my job in downtown Oakland became more drug and crime ridden, it became clear I needed to plan for a future. I knew I didn't want to work in retail, and I began to accept I was headed nowhere. I pulled it together, focused on my studies and became a student with a plan while at Laney Junior College.

Notes

- Late May of 1971 with the Viet Nam War as a backdrop, Marvin Gaye released "What's Going On," perhaps the most iconic album of our generation. Every track was relevant; the environment, young men killed in the war, poverty, neighborhood crime, drugs killing people and destroying families. I saw it, too much, up-close, and personal, daily. I was eighteen.

- From October of 1973 to April of 1974 the Bay Area was gripped by fear as the so-called Zebra killers murdered fifteen people and injured ten others. The serial killers were dubbed the Zebra killers because the men convicted of the crimes were Black and their victims were White. Of course, the heinous nature of the crimes would have captured my attention, but it was more personal because one of the convicted men was a well-loved classmate. Until today he remains in custody and those who know him best and members of his family maintain his innocence.

I HOPED THE HAIR THING WASN'T PROPHETIC

1974 - 1977

It was 1974 and I had amassed enough credits and had a decent enough grade point average to transfer to a four-year college. I was admitted to University of Texas, at Austin. I was awarded Pell grants, Academic Scholarships, and a financial aid package, and off to Austin I went. The reality of it did not hit until I boarded the plane. My brother and sister-in-law took me to the airport. After making sure I was on board my brother came back to speak to me one last time just before takeoff (you could do that back then). Years later he told me when he asked the stewardess where I was seated after he gave her a description of me to make it easier, she said "oh, she's the one crying." I cried all the way from to San Francisco to Austin. To make matters worse, it was the dog days of summer and when I got off the plane (that was when you got off the plane on the tarmac), it was so hot and humid that my hair went back! Hair was so foundational to who I was, I hoped the hair thing wasn't prophetic.

I arrived at UT several weeks before the semester

started as my first financial aid job was Orientation Advisor. For three weeks, four days a week we led orientation sessions for incoming freshmen and transfer students. The program was extensive, full days and evening sessions. The advisors and new students lived in a dorm mimicking the full college experience. I think it was during those sessions that I realized I had a knack for listening and problem solving, no doubt a precursor to my years in Human Resources. And it was lots of fun. When that assignment was complete, I was given a job in the admissions office, and I also worked part time at the local mall. I settled into my new life in Austin easily.

In December of 1974, my grandmother died. When she died it seemed a certain kind of woman died along with her. She was from a generation of women who selflessly dedicated themselves to others. They placed contributing to the success of a husband's business or career ahead of any personal endeavors. They organized and managed the children and households of others, either an employer's household or often the home of their own son or daughter. At the time I wondered if my grandmother had any regrets or wished she had followed a different path. But on reflection I knew she was happy to do exactly what she had done. When she died my heart broke. My heart broke for me, but it hurt for my mother. Though they lived six hundred miles apart my mother and grandmother had a love and a closeness that is impossible to describe. My mother, an only child, actively loved her mother. They spoke on the telephone every Sunday by appointment and in between if events warranted it. She visited her mother often. Without a reason or the need for an excuse my

mother filled her car with friends and family and off we'd
go for a visit. My grandmother visited us regularly as well.
There was no parent prouder than my grandmother was
of my mother. I will never forget the love between the two
of them, never more apparent than when my mother got
her degrees from Cal. Theirs was a love story without
an end.

I learned many things while living in Texas. The most
lasting lesson I learned watching the Watergate hearings
on television. Ordinarily I would have had only had a
passing interest in political events, but this was historic;
the sitting president had allegedly broken several laws.
While that aspect was interesting, it was Congresswoman
Barbara Jordan who captured and held my attention and
the attention of the nation and perhaps the world. She
was extraordinary. She had none of the traditional attrib-
utes that stereotypically make a woman watchable. She
was not what was expected; she was not blonde, she was
not petite, she was not retiring or coy, and she did not
defer to anyone. Her command of the Constitution was
unmatched, her command of language was unmatched,
and the tone and tenor of her voice along with her
bearing made it impossible for me to look away. I was
mesmerized by the events and by Congresswoman
Jordan's mastery of the proceedings.

From Congresswoman Barbara Jordan, I learned that
even when I was not what was expected, I could be
extraordinary.

Academically, I learned discipline and planning while
in Texas. My first semester at UT I was naïve enough to
believe that my haphazard approach to learning would

serve me well. It did not. I got an 'F' for the first time, and it shook me to my core. I had to regroup fast. I could not let anything jeopardize my Academic Scholarships, Pell Grants, or my place at UT. I pulled it together, figured out how to work two jobs, attend class, study, and socialize. I socialized magnificently. Across the quad and across the main drag from the co-op where I lived there was a night club that offered two free drinks to women Monday through Friday nights. I was old enough to drink. I think at that time in Texas everybody over eighteen was old enough to drink. So, we drank (two drinks) and danced, most every night.

While in Texas I learned that I was different. Despite, or because of being different, I made friends, most of whom took delight in my differentness. They were Texans who said "y'all" in a Texas twang and I'm a Californian who says "you guys" in what they claimed was a California accent. People would routinely invite other people to come and "listen to Tina talk."

While in Texas I learned that some people thought I was "not especially Black." I first heard it from the mother of a White friend when she gasped and said it in a whisper that was intended to be heard. "At least she's not especially Black," she declared, signaling her relief. Others said it as a compliment, "You have such a pretty complexion, not especially Black." And others offered it as just a statement of fact, "You know you aren't especially Black." I did my best to leave all that where it belonged.

While in Texas I learned what generational wealth looked like. I had classmates whose families were in the oil business. I mean they had actual oil wells. Along with that kind of wealth went girls with first names like Kennedy and Courtney, who were chauffer driven and wore real fur in winter and real diamonds all the time.

While in Texas, working in the electronics department at Montgomery Ward, I learned that some men felt it was their right to say out loud most anything they were thinking. Because "the customer is always right" they were right even when they were dead wrong. I learned to mitigate situations, find a work around, just as I had seen my parents do.

Notes

- As I was finalizing my plans to go to Texas, in February of 1974 Patty Hearst was kidnapped by a radical group intent on "killing the capitalist state." Her father, William Randolph Hearst was an icon in publishing and at the helm of major syndicated newspapers. The story was front page news across the nation. Patty Hearst is a year younger than I am. At the time she was a college student living in an apartment with her boyfriend in Berkeley. Along with most everybody else, her story caught my attention.

In 1975 the FBI captured the group who kidnapped her. Between the time she was kidnapped and their capture, Patty Hearst allegedly joined the cause, including taking part in an armed bank robbery. At trial, her lawyers claimed she had been brainwashed. She was found guilty and ordered to serve seven years in prison. She had served two years when President Carter commuted her sentence.

She was later pardoned. I often wondered if her White wealth played a part in the decisions. Still do.

- The Viet Nam War ended in May of 1975. Hundreds of thousands American and Vietnamese soldiers and Vietnamese civilians were killed during the war. Villages were left in ruin. Former friends and classmates who had fought in the war came home to hostility and neglect. Some carry mental or physical scars from which they will never recover. So many of them were Black men who had voluntarily served a country where they would forever be underserved.

TIME TO LIVE THE LIFE WE PREPARED FOR

1977-1982

And just like that, it was May of 1977 and my time at UT was done. My friends and I graduated. It was time to live the life we had prepared for. Most of us got jobs that required us to trade our African dashikis and African dresses for blazers and well-fitting slacks. We had to set aside our African jewelry for small gold hoops or studs. And for acceptance in the workplace, we replaced our afros with the corporate haircut and settled into our sameness.

I graduated in Austin in early May, got married at my mother's church on July 16th in Berkeley, and moved to San Jose when we returned from our wedding trip a few days later. I got my first post-college job at Barclay's Bank in September of the same year. After a few months I realized banking was not for me when as Vault Teller I misplaced ten thousand dollars and luckily found it just minutes before they had to alert the FBI.

A few months later in April 1978 I joined Intel where I spent nearly twenty years of a rewarding Human

Resources career. I learned a lot at Intel. Early in my career while working late in the office, a senior executive stopped at my desk and asked how long I had been with the company, I replied several months. He offered what turned out to be among the best advice I have ever gotten, "commit only to what you can reasonably deliver, and once you say you are going to do something, do it." Easy access to all levels of management, Intel University, on-site career related courses offered during the workday, and hands-on experience provided me with a full career tool kit. I took full advantage of everything available to me.

Comingling the responsibilities of marriage and career was tricky, but I had people in my corner. People who gave me practical advice and honest feedback made a world of difference. Some days things worked out spectacularly, other days I failed at work and at home. Thankfully, on balance, the successes outweighed the failures.

At Intel I learned how to "disagree and commit." Whenever a major shift in strategy or a new program was developed before it was implemented the stakeholders were given the opportunity to voice their opinions. There were plenty of times that plans went back to the drawing board or were scrapped based on bottoms up feedback. But if it was decided that the proposal would be implemented, the practice was to commit to fully support the plan. It works everywhere. Either you're in or you're out.

Before we had children, like everyone else, I already had a full plate; work, marriage, and extended family consumed most of my time and attention. Civic issues or politics were not on my radar. Other than exercising my right to vote, I was not politically inclined. Like most

people I took it for granted when things went well or at
least went okay and only became concerned when an
issue negatively impacted me or my family. In 1981 when
President Reagan signed a bill to permanently close feder-
ally funded mental facilities, my sister had been battling
schizophrenia for over a decade. The newly signed bill
placed the responsibility for mental health care in the
hands of the individual states. From my vantage point
California, no doubt like most states, did not have plans in
place to handle the onslaught of the myriad of patient
needs. My mother faced monumental complexities
dealing with bureaucracy and an adult child with schizophrenia who also had legal rights. My mother struggled to
get help for my sister. The law says that unless or until a
person is a threat to him/herself or others, there is
nothing to be done on their behalf or done to avoid the
obvious eventualities. Sadly, we found, by the time a
threat is apparent it's often too late. There was a lack of
resources available in South Berkeley and a lack of refer-
rals. No matter what pressing problems needed attention
the issue of race always seemed to bubble just beneath the
surface. Only a person of color wonders silently if situations happen because of bias and subsequently tries to
convince themselves that bias is not the reason.

During it all the only thing my siblings and I could
offer my mother was moral support and the tacitly agreed
upon practice of keeping our problems to ourselves.

Notes
   - At Intel I learned that fact-based arguments win the

day. One day I found a list of employees in the organization including my peers, with details of past performance ratings, college degree information, and current pay. On inspection I discovered that people without a college degree, less related experience and lower performance ratings were at a higher pay grade and made substantially more money than I. It was not lost on me that all of them were White. But everybody was White, so that was a different problem. Rather than go after the issue as a race-based issue, which, again, I hoped it wasn't, and if it was, impossible to prove, I successfully argued for a fix to my level and compensation using only the facts. At that time, I learned that it pays to have mentors. So, I got myself some. As a result, many people have enhanced my life in many ways. It is my pleasure to return the favor whenever I can.

- By the time the government declared a Crack Epidemic in 1981, Black communities had already been devastated. Crack addicts combined with homeless mental patients changed the trajectory of Black neighborhoods perhaps forever.

- In 1982, Tom Bradley, who was Black, served successfully as mayor of Los Angeles for twenty years. He ran for Governor against Attorney General Deukmejian. It was a very tight race. On election night we went to bed assured by the exit polls that Bradley had won, only to find the next morning he had not. The candidate voters claimed they had voted for, was not in fact who they did vote for. Maybe they were ready for Bradley as Mayor but were not quite ready for Bradley as Governor. We told ourselves that maybe their un-readiness had nothing to do with his Blackness. I was old enough to know better.

WHEN THEY WERE ONLY A PROMISE
1983 - 1987

Our children were born in 1983 and 1987. In addition to their father, they are my greatest joy. Before they were born, I was terrified of having children. I had watched my mother as two of her long-stemmed roses lost their bright future to mental illness. I watched and ineptly tried to help as my mother sidestepped the reality as she tried to advocate for them. I watched as her light dimmed. As a result, I convinced myself that if I didn't have children, I would be okay with it. But God knew the truth and fulfilled His plans. I fell in love with each of my children when they were only a promise.

After the children were born, I continued to work full time at Intel. I was one of the fortunate ones, I have a supportive husband and extended family and we had a network of kind and loving care givers for our children. My job required long hours and a fair amount of travel. Like most people, I juggled my responsibilities. Some days I succeeded and others I failed spectacularly. On balance, the successes outweighed the failures.

The 1980s were difficult personally and professionally. Not long after giving birth to her son, a colleague who was also a friend, flew to Los Angeles on what was to be a one-day business trip. So that she would not be away from her family overnight her plan was to fly out early in the morning and return the same day in the early evening. She never made it, she died in a plane crash on her way home. The crash was shown over and over on the news as it was supposed to be a routine, one hour and fifteen-minute flight, as usual, filled-to-capacity, bringing people home after a days' work. My friend and I had much in common. In addition to our chosen careers and shared friends, she had a son the same age as mine, at the time of her death, just over a year old. That was thirty-six years ago. I think about her still.

When I signed up to be an HR person, I had no idea that one day I would be on a call to a well-loved and respected employee's parents telling them that their son had died in a car accident while on a business trip. That call and his memorial service are days I likely will never forget. I can hear the Vice President of Sales and Marketing saying to the employee's parents, "he loved us, and we loved him back." Out of nowhere I think about it still.

During my career I fired a lot of employees, too many employees. It comes with the responsibility of being a manager. Just as you have the pleasure of hiring people for their dream job, there's also the unfortunate flipside. You are doubly involved when you are an HR manager, sometimes the employee being fired works in the HR group you manage and other times they work within the organizations to which you provide HR support. Either way you're involved and it's difficult. When procedures were followed and employees were given time and resources to improve their performance and they didn't, I was able to reconcile it when the process ended in termination. But I was never able to reconcile sitting across from an employee to tell them they were being laid off through no fault of their own. Even with fair selection criteria and fact-based discussions, the decisions were difficult. The bottom line was people were out of a job. Fairly early in my career Intel had its first big layoff. I sat across the table and had to tell men and women who I knew were husbands, wives, fathers, mothers, and primary breadwinners they were no longer needed. I knew that when we finished our talk they would go home and tell their family they no longer had a job. I think about their reactions still.

In summer of 1984, my father died, he was sixty-six. He was a hard drinker and a light smoker. He smoked at most three or four cigarettes a day, Camels, the unfiltered ones. For all the years of his career he was a carpenter, he worked in Berkeley and around the Bay Area.

I remember before he moved out of our family home, when I was a little girl, his workday started early and as a result he would usually take a nap before dinner. While he slept, sometimes a cigarette hung between his lips with the ash growing. I enjoyed watching the delicate balance. Before the ash fell, I would quietly remove the cigarette from his lips, and he would open his eyes ever so slightly and smile.

Part of his work uniform was a long-sleeved khaki

colored shirt with a flapped breast pocket that closed with a button. Whenever I needed a dollar or two for some particularly important reason, I would quietly open the flap, remove the dollars from his pocket while he napped, and he would open his eyes ever so slightly and smile.

Just before he moved out of the house, in the evenings while he was preparing to go out, he would stand in the bathroom with the door slightly open, wearing t-shirt and trousers. He looked in the mirror as he shaved, he whistled, and I smiled. I didn't know that his going out in the evening was a precursor to him eventually going out and not coming back.

When my father died, selfishly, my heart broke for me. I wished I had known him better. Still do. I have memories of my own, but my fondest memories are of him with my little brother. From the time my little brother could walk, he and my father were a team of two. It made me wish we had had that kind of relationship but still, it warmed my heart. Still does.

When he died my heart hurt, but it broke for my mother. It was impossible not to look at the loss through her lens. It was so final, done. Whatever their relationship was, with his death, the relationship was all it would ever be, or so I thought. Spending time with my mother as she planned for my father's burial, I learned things about her that I could not possibly have imagined. She loved baseball, who knew? She prayed for Daryl Strawberry, a well-known player for the New York Mets. As my mother selected flowers for the service, I learned from the florist that she had flowers placed at the altar every Sunday during the birth month of my father and each of her children. At the mortuary I learned that my parent's relationship would continue throughout eternity. While planning my father's funeral my mother arranged for the two of them to be buried in a double-decker grave.

Years after my father died a cousin sent my father's second grade class photo, taken in Kentucky where he was born and raised. Looking at the picture I was struck by the fact that the little boy in that old photo, like us all, had no idea where life would take him. Little did he know he would grow up, leave Kentucky, move to the South side of Chicago, where he would meet and marry a woman who only he would call by her middle name from the day they met until he closed his eyes for the last time. Little did he know by the time he was twenty-five he would move to Berkeley, California where he knew no one, buy a home on Julia Street, where he would build a second story and apartments in back with his own hands for his family, where his wife would live until she closed her eyes for the last time. Little did he know; he would leave this life at just sixty-six, leaving six children whose lives were immeasurably enriched by his decision to leave Chicago. Little did I know that I'd wish I'd told him so.

My father died in summer of 1984, just seven years after he walked me down the aisle and just one year after my first child was born. Our son barely remembers him, and our daughter never met him.

Notes

- In 1985 Sally Field won an Oscar for her role in Places
in the Heart. In her acceptance speech she has been
misquoted as saying "You like me, you really like me."
What she really said was "Right now, you like me." The
difference is subtle yet profound. In 1985, right then, at
that moment, the race issue seemed less of an issue. At
that moment it seemed White people liked us. What was
not to like when all was right with their world? In January
of 1985 President Reagan was sworn in for his second term
promising "Morning in America." The economy was
making steady gains. Technology was improving the way
business and basic communications were handled. The
future looked bright, and the pie was big enough for
everyone to have at least a sliver. It seemed everybody
liked everybody. We, the Affirmative Action generation
had our sliver of the American pie. We had been thriving
in our careers for over a decade and steadily moving up
the career ladder. Our 2.5 children were well situated. Our
marriages were blissful. Our parents were self-sustaining.
All was right with our world, so despite history we
convinced ourselves White America liked us, they really
liked us.

- On January 28, 1986, 8:39 am, we were casually
assembled in the cafeteria at work. A television had been
brought in for the occasion. We were chatting quietly
until we heard the countdown to blast off begin. We
joined in, until we heard the reporter say, "there's something wrong." A hush fell over the cafeteria as the Chal-
lenger exploded before our eyes. Indescribable is the only
word I can think of. One minute we were filled with

excitement and wonder as we watched the diverse seven-member crew that included a Black man, two women, one of whom was a teacher, as they boarded the shuttle. The next minute was indescribable. We stood transfixed, bound by grief.

SADNESS FELL ON THE FOURS

1974, 1984, 1994

Decade after decade, sadness fell on the fours. My grand-mother died in 1974. My father died in 1984. My mother died in 1994. Each death brought grief and lessons. Among the lessons, I learned ten years is not long enough to recover, nothing prepares you for the death of your mother and death is final.

Before my mother died, I worried about many things, thankfully most never happened. But I never worried about my mother. She was formidable, perennial, time-less. She was inextricably woven into the fabric of my life and the lives of so many. It never occurred to me that she might die. And her death was without preamble. We didn't know she was sick until the afternoon my sister and me joined her for what we thought was a routine doctor visit to be followed by a late lunch. It was then that we learned she had advanced stage cancer and within days she was admitted into the hospital. After several days they determined there was nothing further they could do, and she was sent home. The day after she came home a visiting nurse told us, "If people would like to see your mother, tell them not to tarry." I didn't know exactly what tarry meant. Later that day I looked it up. It means delay, she was telling us don't delay. My tears fell as reality and the enormity of it set in.

Days later she was gone, and my siblings and I became members of a club none of us wanted to join. There were days that my heart hurt, with a physical pain that came over me and took my breath away. Then one day the pain was gone and in its place is an intense longing. I long for my mother as she was when she was at her best. Playing records, telling stories, welcoming all visitors. I long to hear my mother's voice as she explains the intricacies of the notes of one of her favorite songs, hear her laugh at a story she has told many times before but each time we are delighted by the way she tells it. I long to smell the scent of her favorite perfume. Even now when I smell it in a crowd, I look for her.

I long for the matched set, three boys and three girls; the first four, then Tina, then Tony. I long to hear her call us "her half dozen long stemmed roses."

IMPOSSIBLE TO REIMAGINE OR IGNORE

1990S - 2000S

And just like that, in the late 90s I left my corporate life behind. It had been a wild ride filled with opportunity, challenge, and reward. But every silver lining has a cloud, and the clouds were sometimes very dark. When I left, I never looked back.

Finding my rhythm, I was content puttering around the house until I wasn't. It was at that time that I made a commitment to volunteerism, a commitment I continue to honor. Among other venues, I volunteered weekly at The Career Closet until they closed their doors. Our mission was to prepare underserved women for job interviews, many were re-entering the workforce or had never held a job. We also provided them workplace-appropriate clothing for their first week at work.

I had no idea the need was so vast, and the stories so sad. I met women who were ten times smarter than I but had started life with the deck stacked against them. Over time, circumstances had piled up rendering their chances for success slim. But their perseverance and strong survival instincts buoyed and sustained them. In working with these women, I regularly reached for and held dear words my mother often said to me, "Where there's life there's hope." I was comforted whenever she said it. I still am.

During that time, our family life was kid-centric, our friends and associates were in the same phase of life and had similar goals and values. We didn't see it, but we were in a bubble, a harmonious, homogeneous bubble. As adults, as parents, none of us really knew what we were doing, but every day we did our best, making it up as we went along. As a result, the days were often long, but looking back the years were very short. More details on that will have to come from the books our children write.

Life outside of our bubble didn't get much of my attention, I fell into a pattern of benign disinterest. Because things were going mostly according to plan it never occurred to me to do anything other than what I was doing. I continued in that way for years. I peeked out of the bubble only when something outside became impossible to reimagine or ignore.

Notes

- In March of 1991 Rodney King, suspected drunk driver, led officers on an eight-mile high-speed chase that ended with him being beaten by twenty-four police officers. The officers were charged with assault and after a trial acquitted.

"Why can't we all just get along?" is the famous quote attributed to Rodney King. It is a misquote. What he really said was "Can't we all get along?" It is a subtle yet profound difference. The misquote is a rhetorical question, but the actual quote is a call to action. A call that has yet to be answered.

- October 3,1995 After a lengthy trial OJ Simpson, charged with murder was acquitted. The verdict was polarizing in the Black community, with strong feelings on both sides. And some felt Simpson was guilty of the crimes but because the judicial system is inherently unfair to Black men, they were okay with the outcome, sort of evening the score. I felt if there were any silver bullets to right past wrongs, it was a shame to waste one on him.

- April 20,1999 Columbine massacre. Two high school seniors shot and killed twelve classmates and one teacher. They injured twenty-one of their classmates. Columbine is often seen as iconic, as unleashing an insidious form of evil that it is perpetrated when least expected, at school, in a movie theater, during worship service, in the work-place. An evil that has yet to be contained.

- November 7, 2000, Hanging chads. Despite the hotly contested, highly subjective review of the hanging chads on cast ballots, Republican candidate George W. Bush narrowly won the election. Democrats accepted the results and life went on.

. . .

- September 11, 2001, Terrorist attacks. The devastation and the impact to our sense of well-being is beyond words.

- August 29, 2005, Hurricane Katrina. On its face the hurricane was an act of nature, but the government response was an act of neglect. Hurricane Katrina and the government response reenforced the precariousness of being poor in America, and the tragedy of being poor and Black in America. There are people and neighborhoods that have yet to recover.

I KNEW BETTER

By 2007 our homogenous, harmonious bubble was nearly non-existent. Our children were finishing college and life circumstances had pulled us in different directions. Our support for and belief in Barack Obama created a new bubble. On November 4th, 2008, Barack Obama became the 44th President of the United States. With his election, like others in our new bubble, I chose to believe or at least hope the issue of race had finally been put to bed. Like others in our new bubble, instead of acknowledging the historical facts about race in America, I reached for the promise of facts not yet in evidence. Besides, I told myself, America had other demons to face. But I knew better.

Whenever I peek outside of our new bubble, I see a steady march back in time, revisiting forms of hate and bigotry that have historically lurked just below the surface.

Notes

- February 26, 2012, Trayvon Martin was murdered while walking home from a convenience store. His killer was acquitted when the jury bought into the defense theory that they too would be afraid of a boy who looked like him, walking in their neighborhood, wearing a hoodie. Trayvon Martin is representative of Black people who are murdered, sometimes at the hands of law enforcement, whose killers are not held accountable.

- November 7, 2012, President Barack Obama was elected to serve a second term. This time I had no illusions as unbridled hatred was sucking the oxygen from our bubble. Despite or because we had a Black president, on the daily, it was clear the issue of race was in no way solved in America. It was impossible to reimage or ignore the language used by some to describe the occupants of the White House or their opinion of the job the president was doing. Two things were true at the same time; I was thrilled to have Barack Obama and his family in the White House, but I was terrified to have Barack Obama and his family in the White House.

2015

On June 15, 2015, the one term, twice impeached former president announced his then candidacy for president of the United States.

2016

- November 8, 2016, Hillary Clinton won the popular vote but lost the electoral college vote and the election.

2017

- August 12, 2017, Charlottesville, Va. "Very fine people on both sides." Young White males marched through the streets during the night carrying torches shouting, "Jews will not replace us." Counter-protesters rebuked them. The then president responded by declaring there were "very fine people on both sides."

2019

- December 18, 2019, Quid pro quo. The US House impeached the sitting president.

2020

- February 2020, Covid 19 shut down the whole world for months. The sitting president and his administration dismissed it as a minor threat and then as a political hoax. To date 625,000 Americans have died from Covid 19.

- February 5, 2020, The US Senate acquit the sitting president of impeachment charges.

- May 25th George Floyd was murdered by a police officer as the whole world watched, triggering protests nationwide and in locations around the world. People took to the streets in protest for months.

- November 3rd Joe Biden was elected 46th President of the United States. His running mate, Kamala Harris, was elected 49th Vice President. The one term, twice impeached former president did not concede defeat but instead asserted the election was stolen. As of this writing that assertion continues to be made by 45th president and his supporters.

WILL THEY WANT IT
NOW. 2021

At the start of the new year, we were hopeful. More so this year. There was a new administration and a Covid vaccine on the horizon. Like so many retired people we had taken the admonition to shelter in place literally. For almost a year we went out only when necessary. Our world shrank to the size of our home. Quite unnatural for sixty-some-things who are accustomed to affiliating with groups, traveling and socializing. But we are among the lucky ones whose lives did not fundamentally change. While we are going out more often now, we continue to rely on Facebook and Zoom meetings to bring a sense of normalcy.

Like so many parents, we watched helplessly as our children's world shrank to the size of their homes. Quite unnatural for thirty-somethings who are used to traveling, mingling, and socializing indiscriminately. Many of our children can do their jobs from home, isolated from family, colleagues, and friends. Many others face life on the front lines putting their personal safety at risk every day. We also watch as our children figure it out. They make the best of the circumstances and maintain a rich social life through Instagram, Google Hangouts, Tiny Desk Concerts, Versus, and others that I know nothing about. We have all created literal bubbles, included are people we trust with our lives. The jury is out on how all of this will affect us.

We are more than half-way through the year and fifty-six percent of Republicans continue to believe the 2020 election was stolen. Though the vaccine has been available for months only forty-eight percent of eligible Americans are fully vaccinated. There is an uneasy détente between the vaccinated and the unvaccinated, the masked and the unmasked. In some cases, the decision to get the vaccine or wear a mask is connected to a political party affiliation.

As of June 15th, California was fully reopened. But we are changed. The world is changed. And the life we so carefully planned for ourselves, and our children may no longer exist. And if it does, will they want it?

Note

More than anything I miss going about my business with a casual ease.

Sharing smiles with strangers, just as random as I please.

I miss turning on the TV assuming everything is good.

I miss crowding into spaces, probably closer than we should.

I miss thinking the best of others, assuming they think the best of me.

I miss taking things for granted, assuming that's how they'd always be.

But that was then and now is now, so I'll do exactly as we're told.

And I'll do my best to do my best to keep our world from growing cold.

When seeing things as they are, maybe it's oblivion I miss.

But as experience teaches time and again, ignorance really isn't bliss.

EPILOGUE

TODAY. JULY 30, 2021

"We do not write to be understood; we write to understand." C. Day-Lewis

To fully understand the gifts of the present and the promises of the future, it's necessary to look back at the realities of the past. Writing 'It Happened on Our Watch' triggered an avalanche of emotions, high highs, and low lows. It forced me to face what it means to be a citizen of this great country, acknowledging that we have faced challenges and benefited from opportunities that are beyond the average imagination. Looking back has been dizzying and humbling.

No doubt every generation judges itself harshly as the baton is clumsily passed. No doubt every generation looks at the next with a combination of trepidation and awe. But I submit, on balance, I look at our successors with unmitigated awe.

Earlier I asked, do our children want the life we

planned for them? Perry Mason would say, "That question is incompetent, irrelevant, and immaterial." The very notion is a bit arrogant and self-serving. There is a much better question. Why would they want the life we planned for them? Like the generations who came before them, they are creating a life that is so much better.

ABOUT THE AUTHOR

Award-winning author, Tina Jones Williams, A Reasonable Woman, has written eight books which pay homage
to the rich traditions in the African American community.
Born and raised in the all-black neighborhood on Julia
Street in South Berkeley, Tina attended neighborhood
schools until seventh grade when she was bussed out of
her area to become a member of the first desegregated
junior high school in Berkeley. Tina attended Berkeley
High, the only public high school in town.

   After high school graduation, Tina went to the University of Texas, at Austin where she earned a B.A. degree in
Business/General & Comparative Studies. The lure of
family brought her back to the Bay Area where she
married, settled in Silicon Valley, and had a career in the

Tech Industry. She is still happily married (to the same man) and the mother of two adult children who are the apples of her eye. She is close to her siblings, extended family and delights in her friendships.

Since publishing her Julia Street Series, Tina has led bi-annual neighborhood walks which begin and end on Julia Street where the four books are set. During the walks, Tina shares anecdotes, folklore, and history about times, places, and people she feels should not be forgotten. As a result of her books and neighborhood walks, Tina is pictured on a South Berkeley mural reflecting the city's history. Julia Street is also depicted on the mural and is listed among ten streets considered the "heart of South Berkeley."

Tina is a proud and active member of Alpha Kappa Alpha Sorority, Inc., the oldest African American Sorority with an international membership of more than 300,000 college-educated women committed to a lifetime of service to ALL mankind. She is a contributor to the Berkeley Historical Society and the South Berkeley Legacy Project. She is a member of the National League of American Pen Women and a literacy and career coach.

Reach Tina at areasonablewoman@aol.com

TINA JONES WILLIAMS
Author
A REASONABLE WOMAN

It Happened on Our Watch

The Julia Street Series:

All's Well That Ends- Prequel

Sara's Song -Book 1

Dance or Get Out - Book 2

Perfect Pitch - Book 3

The Bridge to Freedom Series:

For Their Convenience - Book 1

On Closer Inspection - Book 2

A Delicate Balance - Book 3

Stand alone:

Some Things I Want You to Know

The Julia Street series

From Book I: *Sara's Song: Bolstered by Hope ... a segregated train ride is only the beginning.*

More than anything Sara hoped her life on Julia Street would be a sweet melody, but fate had more of a haunting refrain in mind.

After leaving Chicago behind, Sara and husband Ben Jameson settled into an all Black South Berkeley working-class neighborhood that sat in the shadow of the affluent East Berkeley Hills. They had left behind everyone and everything they knew and loved to go to a place they had never been. Armed with hope, Sara and family faced two wars, social injustice, economic challenges, personal sorrow, and harsh life lessons. Ultimately, they were defined by their unflagging hope, enduring friendships, strong neighborhood connections, and opportunities beyond their wildest dreams.

Sara's Song, The Julia Street Series Book 1 lovingly spans 1940's - 1960's.

The Bridge to Freedom series

From Book 1: **A lot can happen in ten days …**

For domestic worker Violet Banks,the party dragged on. When guests had enough to drink to blame their actions on the alcohol, the women began touching Violet's hair, her skin, even her uniform, as they overtly called out all the things that made her different.Their husbands covertly tried to touch her while whispering all the things they hoped made them alike. Not all of them behaved this way, some were even silently sympathetic; averting their eyes and shaking their heads. But this time it was too much, and Violet knew what she did next would change the course of her life forever.

For Their Convenience,Book 1 Bridge to Freedom Series

Tina Jones Williams
Author, Storyteller, Folklorist

Take a walk down memory lane;
remembering people, places and times
which should not be forgotten.

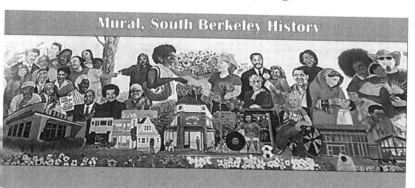

Mural, South Berkeley History

Made in the USA
Las Vegas, NV
13 September 2021